Revelation

A VISUAL JOURNEY WHAT DID JOHN SEE?

ISAIAS GUEVARA

All Scripture quotations are taken from the authorized King James Version.

REVELATION: WHAT DID JOHN SEE?

ISBN 0-9763800-3-X
Printed in China
© 2005 by Isaias Guevara

Isaias Guevara, Illustrator
321 W. Birch
Fresno, CA 93650

Orison Publishers
PO Box 188
Grantham, PA 17027
Ph: 717-433-7985   Fax: 717-427-1525

1 2 3 4 5 6 7 8 9 10 / 11 10 09 08 07 06 05

Dedications

I want to dedicate this book to my Lord Jesus Christ,
the Author of my soul, who has
inspired me to draw every picture. *HALLELUJAH!*

To my beautiful wife Jenny Guevara, who supported
me through the entire project; I love you.
And to my four lovely daughters Brenetta, Deborah,
Ireyna, and little Joyce.

A special thanks to my mother-in-law, my brothers-in-law,
my sister-in-law, and her husband. My sister,
her husband, all my brothers, my nieces, their husbands,
and Pilar Garcia for their great support.

To my dad Bolivar Guevara,
who has done so much to serve God.
He has taught me to love and to keep God's Word
a great man of God.

And a very special thanks to my pastors
G.L. and Jackie Johnson for the encouragement
they gave me. Thank you very much.

Contents

Foreword

I am thrilled to have been asked to add a word to the very considerable
task of my dear friend, Isaias Guevara.

I have known the Guevara family for 25 years or more, and I have found them to be
unusually talented, unusually committed to our Lord Jesus, and exemplary
in their family life. You will be inspired as you see and study Isaias' insights
in these illustrations of the truths in the Book of Revelation.

I commend it to you and pray it will be a blessing.

G.L. Johnson
Senior Pastor, Peoples Church: A Place Called Home! – Fresno, CA

Introduction

When I was a teenager, our father taught us from the Book of Revelation.
In my heart there rose a passion to know more about the end of the world.
This built up my faith in God.

This project is on the entire Book of Revelation;
no interpretation has been added.

The purpose of this book is to enable the reader to visualize everything
just as the apostle John saw it. This book contains 171 original drawings.
All who have seen it, especially my pastor, have been deeply blessed.

I pray that this book will be a blessing to both the churched and the un-churched.
Young and old will be able to understand and enjoy the Revelation as well.

I truly believe these illustrations give a good idea of John's visions
for everyone to study. I pray this book will be a blessing to your life.

Isaías Guevara

I heard behind me a great voice Revelation 1:1-11

Seven Golden
Candlesticks
Revelation 1:12-16

Out of His mouth went a sharp, two-edged sword Revelation 1:16

I fell at His feet as dead Revelation 1:17-3:22

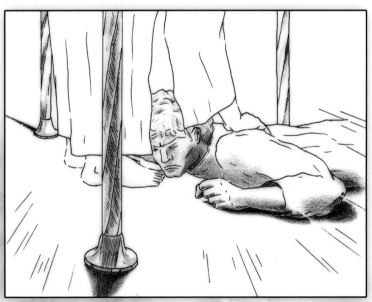

A door was
opened in heaven
Revelation 4:1

A throne
set in
heaven
Revelation
4:2-4

Seven lamps
of fire
Revelation 4:5

A sea of glass Revelation 4:6

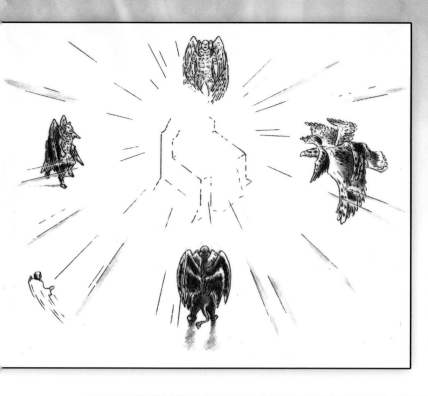

Four beasts
full of eyes
Revelation 4:6-8

hey cast
their
crowns
fore the
throne
Revelation
4:9-11

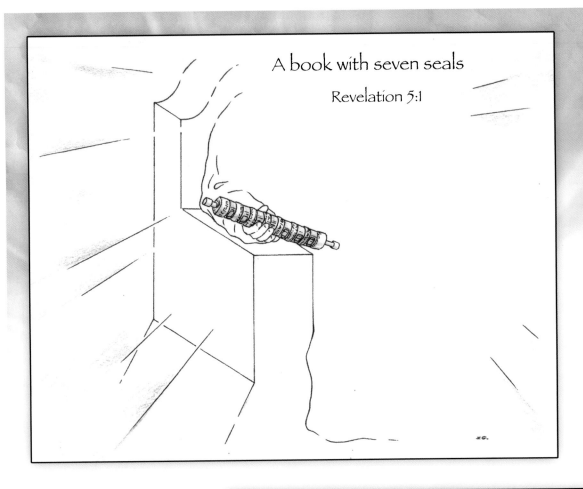

A book with seven seals

Revelation 5:1

A strong angel
proclaiming
Revelation 5:2

I wept much

Revelation 5:3-4

One of
the elders

Revelation 5:5

A Lamb standing Revelation 5:6

He took the book

Revelation 5:7

They fell down
before the Lamb
Revelation 5:8-10

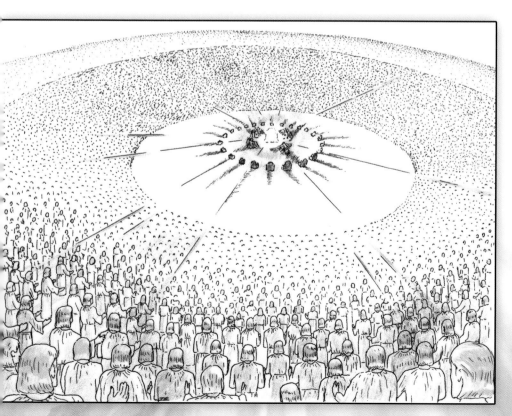

Thousands
of angels
Revelation 5:11-13

The four beasts said Amen

Revelation 5:14

The first seal

Revelation 6:1-2

The second seal

Revelation 6:3-4

The third seal

Revelation 6:5-6

The fourth seal

Revelation 6:7-8

The fifth seal

Revelation 6:9-11

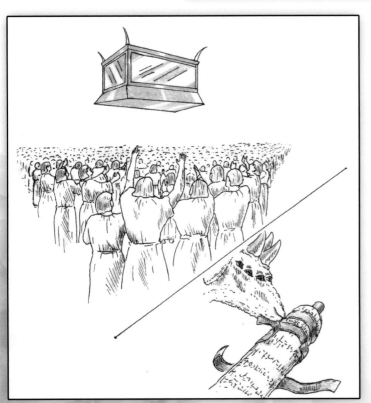

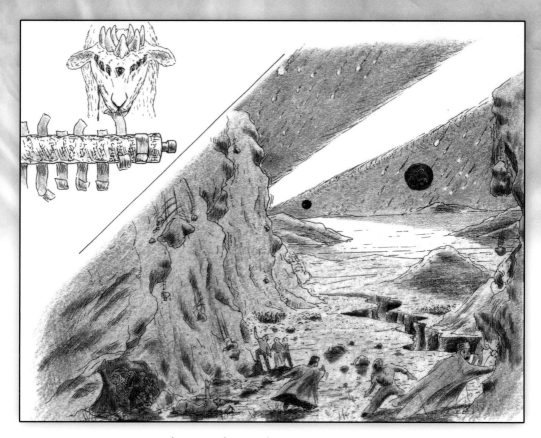

The sixth seal Revelation 6:12-17

Four angels at
the four corners
of the earth
Revelation 7:1-8

A great
multitude
holding palm
branches
Revelation 7:9-10

They fell
down and
worshipped
God
Revelation
7:11-12

One of the
elders asked
me...
Revelation 7:13-17

The seventh
seal
Revelation 8:1

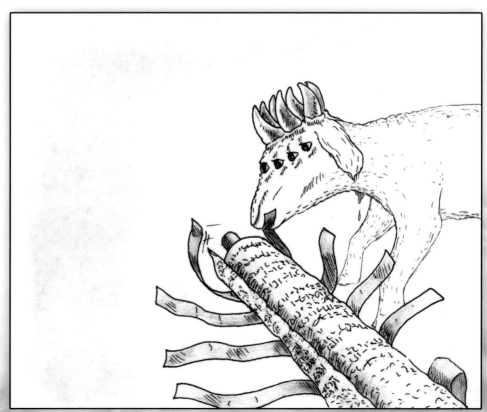

The seven angels with trumpets at the altar Revelation 8:2-4

The angel cast the censer Revelation 8:5-6

The first
trumpet
Revelation 8:7

The second
trumpet
Revelation
8:8-9

17

The sea turned into blood Revelation 8:8-9

The third trumpet
Revelation 8:10-11

The star
is called
Wormwood
Revelation 8:11

The fourth trumpet Revelation 8:12

Flying through
the midst of heaven
Revelation 8:13

The fifth
trumpet
Revelation 9:1

He opened the
bottomless pit
Revelation 9:2

The locusts Revelation 9:3-12

The sixth trumpet

Revelation 9:13-14

The army of horsemen Revelation 9:15-21

The angel
clothed with
a cloud
Revelation 10:1-2

He cried loud, as a lion roareth Revelation 10:3-4

He lifted up his
hand to heaven
Revelation 10:5-7

Take the little book Revelation 10:8-9

I took the little book Revelation 10:10

I ate the little book
Revelation 10:10

You must prophesy Revelation 10:11

A reed like
unto a rod
Revelation 11:1-14

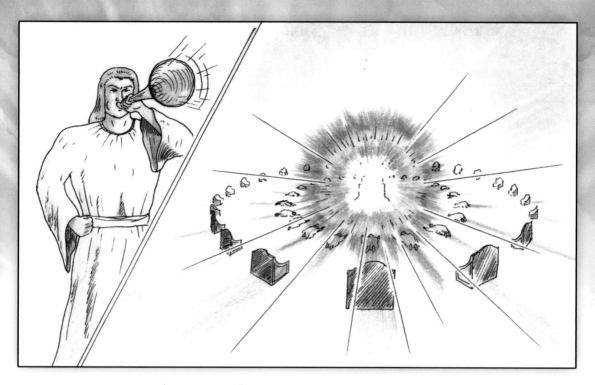

The seventh trumpet Revelation 11:15-18

The temple of
God was opened
Revelation 11:19

A woman
clothed
with the sun
Revelation 12:1-2

A great
red dragon
Revelation
12:3-4

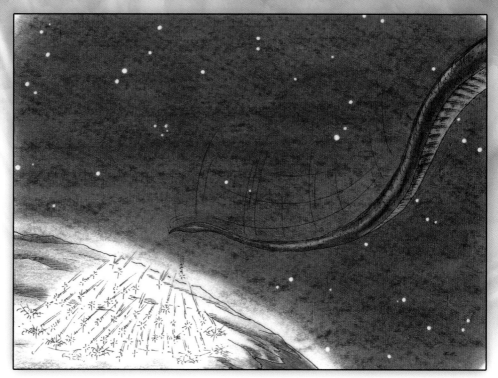

The stars of
heaven cast to
the earth
Revelation 12:4

He gets
ready to
devour
her child
Revelation 12:4

She gave birth

Revelation 12:5

The woman fled

Revelation 12:6

There was war
in heaven
Revelation 12:7

The dragon
and his
angels
cast out
Revelation
12:8-12

He persecuted
the woman
Revelation 12:13

Two wings of a great eagle Revelation 12:14

Out of his mouth water as a flood Revelation 12:15-16

The dragon
went to
make war
Revelation 12:17

The beast
Revelation 13:1-2

The wounded head
Revelation 13:3

34

They worshipped
the dragon and
the beast
Revelation 13:3-10

Another beast
Revelation 13:11

He doeth great
wonders and
deceiveth them
Revelation 13:12-14

The image of
the beast
Revelation 13:14

Gave life unto
the image
Revelation 13:15

The mark
of the
beast
Revelation
13:16-18

144,000 Revelation 14:1-5

Another
angel flies
Revelation 14:6-7

Another angel
followed
Revelation 14:8

A third angel followed Revelation 14:9-12

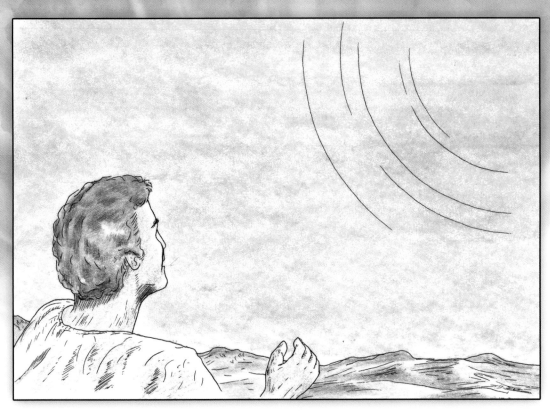

A voice
from
heaven
Revelation
14:13

One sat upon a white cloud Revelation 14:14

Another
angel came out
Revelation 14:15

He thrust in his sickle Revelation 14:16

Another angel came out Revelation 14:17

Another angel
came from
the altar
Revelation 14:18

He thrust his sickle Revelation 14:19

He gathered
the grapes
Revelation 14:19

The great
winepress
Revelation 14:19

The grapes were trampled Revelation 14:20

The seven
last plagues
Revelation 15:1

A sea of glass mixes with fire Revelation 15:2-4

The temple and the seven angels Revelation 15:5-6

The seven
golden vials of
the wrath of God
Revelation 15:7

Smoke filled
the temple
Revelation 15:8

A great voice
out of the
temple
Revelation 16:1

The first vial
Revelation 16:2

The second vial
Revelation 16:3

The third vial Revelation 16:4-7

The fourth vial
Revelation 16:8

Men were scorched Revelation 16:9

The fifth vial
Revelation 16:10-11

The sixth vial
Revelation 16:12

The water was
dried up
Revelation 16:12

Three unclean spirits Revelation 16:13

They gather them
Revelation 16:14-16

The seventh vial
Revelation 16:17

Babylon divided Revelation 16:18-20

The great hail Revelation 16:21

One of the
seven angels
talked with me
Revelation 17:1-2

He carried

me away
Revelation 17:3

A woman sits upon a beast Revelation 17:3-5

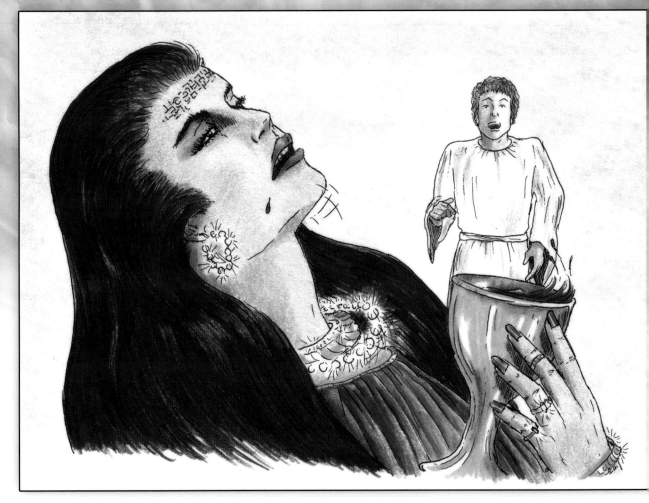

She was drunken with the blood of saints Revelation 17:6

The angel said
unto me...
Revelation 17:7-14

He also said unto me…   Revelation 17:15-18

Another angel
came down
Revelation 18:1

He cried out with a strong voice Revelation 18:2-3

Another voice
from heaven
Revelation 18:4-20

The angel with
the stone
Revelation 18:21-24

He cast the stone into the sea Revelation 18:21-24

I heard a
great voice
Revelation 19:1-3

They fell down and worshipped Revelation 19:4

Amen; Alleluia Revelation 19:4

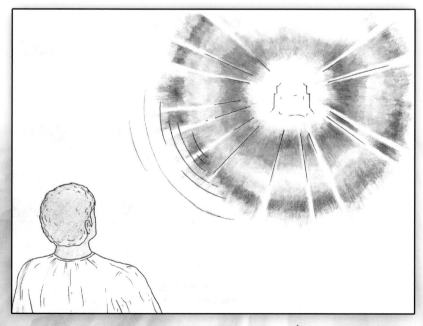

A voice out of
the throne
Revelation 19:5

The voice of a
great multitude
Revelation 19:6-8

The angel
said to me…
Revelation 19:9

I fell at his feet to worship Revelation 19:10

The white horse and He that sat upon him Revelation 19:11-16

63

An angel
standing
in the sun
Revelation 19:17-18

They gather together to make war Revelation 19:19

Both cast alive into a lake of fire Revelation 19:20

Slain with
the sword
Revelation 19:21

All the birds
were filled
Revelation 19:21

A great chain Revelation 20:1

Bound a
thousand years
Revelation 20:2

The bottomless pit Revelation 20:3

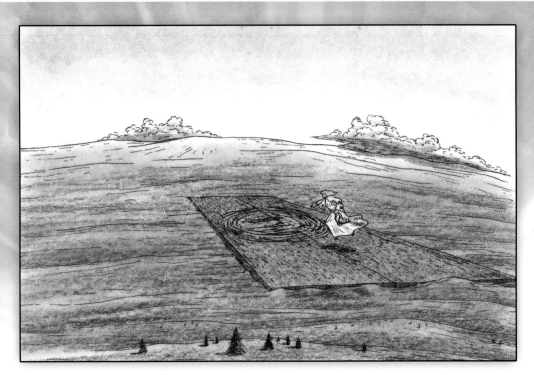

Shut and sealed Revelation 20:3

Thrones Revelation 20:4

Souls Revelation 20:4

They reigned with Christ Revelation 20:4-6

Satan shall be loosed Revelation 20:7-8

He deceives
the nations
Revelation 20:8

The
beloved city
Revelation 20:9

Devoured
by fire
Revelation 20:9

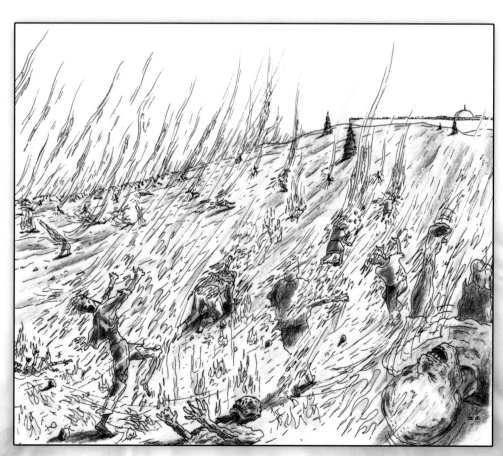

The devil is cast into the lake of fire
Revelation 20:10

Earth and heaven fled away Revelation 20:11

The dead were judged Revelation 20:12

Books were opened Revelation 20:12

The sea, death
and hell gave
up the dead
Revelation 20:13

They were judged Revelation 20:13

Death and hell were cast into the lake of fire Revelation 20:14

Whosoever
was not
found in the
book of life
Revelation 20:15

A new heaven
and a new earth
Revelation 21:1

New Jerusalem Revelation 21:2

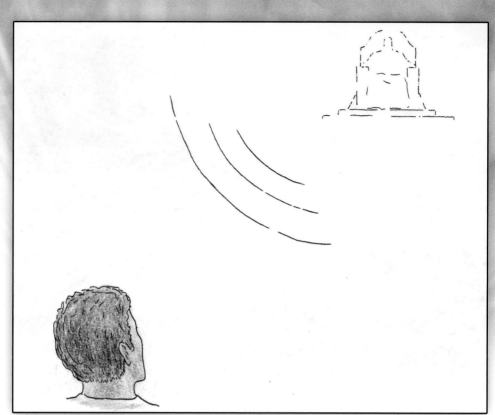

A great voice
Revelation 21:3-4

He that sat upon
the throne said...
Revelation 21:5-8

There came unto
me one of the
seven angels
Revelation 21:9

He showed me that great city Revelation 21:10-11

Great walls
Revelation 21:12-14

A measuring
reed
Revelation 21:15

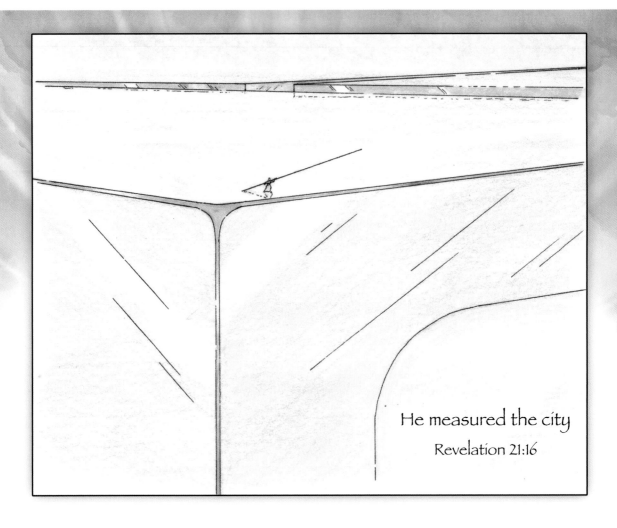

He measured the city
Revelation 21:16

He measured
the wall
Revelation 21:17-18

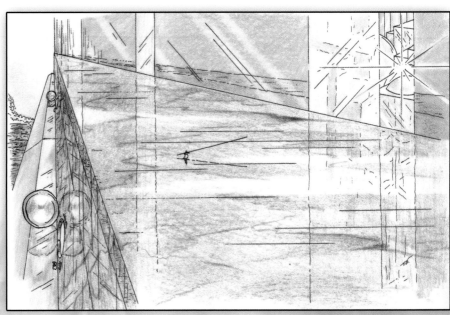

The foundations of the city's wall Revelation 21:19-20

The pearl gates
Revelation 21:21

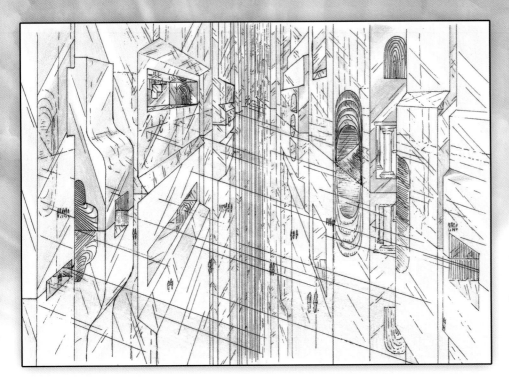

The street
of the city
Revelation 21:21

No need of the sun Revelation 21:22-24

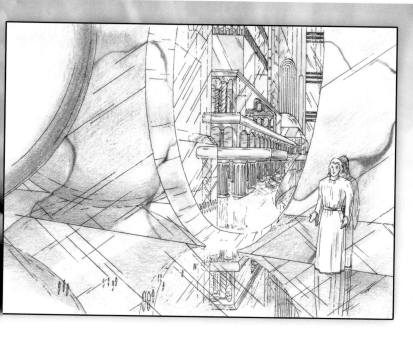

Its gates shall
not be shut
Revelation 21:25-27

A river Revelation 22:1-2

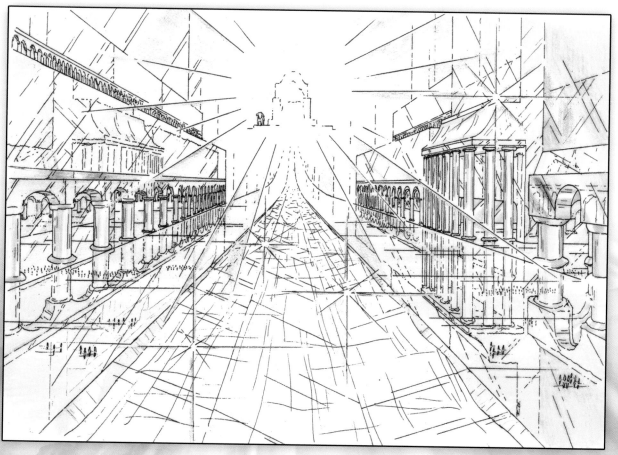

The tree of life Revelation 22:2-5

And he said
unto me…
Revelation 22:6-7

I fell down to worship Revelation 22:8-9

And He said
unto me...
Revelation 22:10-20

Come, Lord Jesus Revelation 22:20-21

The Only Way to Heaven

The Bible says there's only one way to heaven!

"Jesus saith unto him, I am the way, the truth, and the life: no man cometh unto the Father, but by me."

(John 14:6)

"For God so loved the world, that he gave his only begotten Son, that whosoever believeth in him should not perish, but have everlasting life."

(John 3:16)

The Bible also says:

"That if thou shalt confess with thy mouth the Lord Jesus, and shalt believe in thine heart that God hath raised him from the dead, thou shalt be saved."

(Romans 10:9)

What to pray?

"Dear God, I am a sinner and need forgiveness. I believe that Jesus Christ shed His precious blood and died for my sin. I am willing to turn from my sin. I now invite Christ to come into my heart and life as my personal Savior. Amen."

If you trusted Jesus as your Savior, you have just begun a wonderful new life with Him. Now:

1. Read your Bible every day to get to know Jesus Christ better.
2. Talk to God in prayer every day.
3. Be baptized; worship, fellowship, and serve with other Christians in a church where Christ is preached and the Bible is the final authority.
4. Tell others about Jesus Christ.